UNCONDITIONING

A PATH TO FREEDOM

SHAHRUKH AHMED

Made with ♥ on the Notion Press Platform
www.notionpress.com

I dedicate this book to the readers, to those suffering alone. I hope this book guides you toward happiness and freedom.

Contents

Preface

This book is a collection of answers I found for problems we face in daily life. It will start with making you realise the origin of the issues, then introduce each problem with its solutions. It does not claim to treat any neurotic or psychotic problem where seeking medical attention is the answer. It may be a new concept to some, but it might offend others. It may be thought-provoking to some and painful to read for others. I hope it helps you in some way or another.

Acknowledgements

I thank my friends, family and teachers who taught me everything and kept me alive to write this book.

Prologue

To understand this book, you should know what conditioning means.

What happens when we see and smell good food? We start salivating, right?

Our mouth becomes watery, and we start preparing to eat that food even if it is not meant for us. In the same way, animals have a more robust response than us when they see food. Imagine if we developed a habit of salivation if our doorbell started ringing. It is weird, right? But this is possible. A scientist named Pavlov experimented on his dog. He started ringing a bell whenever he gave food to his dog. The dog started wagging its tail and salivating on seeing food meant for him. When this was done for a few days, the dog developed an abnormal response in few days. Pavlov observed that the dog started salivating on ringing the bell even when the food was not there. He called this process conditioning in which a new type of behaviour can be formed in the dog, which is unnatural.

This conditioning happens every day when humans teach and learn to fit in society from their childhood. We evolved from animals. Only a few grams of the brain, its connections and a few genes make us different from other species. We are born with all the qualities to survive. We are animals who have structured themselves into sophisticated beings. This process of becoming a human from an animal who believes in society, relationships, trade, jobs etc, is painful. It takes away our animalness to an extent but leaves us caged into various bonds. Many responses which are developed make an individual fit into the structured society. In this process, there is a high chance that the person loses their identity as a living being.

The idea behind unconditioning is unlearning all this and finding your freedom as an individual again.

CHAPTER ONE

Origin

"I'm convinced that when we help our children find healthy ways of dealing with their feelings, ways that don't hurt them or anyone else. We're making our world a safer, better place - Mr. Rogers"

Mr Fred Rogers was the host of a famous television programme named a beautiful day in the Neighbourhood in 1968. Through this show, he showed the importance of n childhood.

Childhood is supposed to be a happy time. It is when we are vulnerable to anything that happens, whether it is good or bad. Every child should receive care and love from their family, friends, and teachers.

It helps develop qualities like curiosity and self-confidence. Curiosity is important for the initiation of learning something. A curious child wants to learn about their surroundings. Self-confidence is necessary to keep doing the thing that child starts to learn.

Unfortunately, some children, or I would rather be bold to say most of them, do not get the conducive environment, love, and care to develop these qualities in their childhood. Some receive cold treatment from their parents; some even face a trauma from physical assault and sexual abuse.

It is painful to talk about these things, but we must address them despite being difficult here.

Almost all problems start in childhood and haunt us for the rest of our lives. We keep wondering what is wrong with us. It makes us feel that we are not good enough. We keep wondering why we react in such ways, why some situations haunt us but seem normal to others.

What causes these things to happen?

And if they are the result of traumatic childhood experiences.

Why our elders did this to us?

There is a famous dialogue explaining the cause " We are victims of victims." the parents or people who do such things with children are themselves facing mental difficulties. Some are unhappy with their jobs, spouse, or their parents. People who do child abuse in the form of physical assault and sexual abuse are found to be dealing with these problems themselves. Some might have desires that are not being addressed and not allowed by society. Children seem to fall prey to these things as they cannot voice out and rebel like adults.

Does all this justify these deep wounds we give to our children? Of course not.

What can we do to prevent and control these things? Once happen, they have long-lasting impacts.

It isn't my past; it is my present - Helena Wilson

Any unpleasant situation where you lose control leaves a traumatic experience. We are still determining the difficulty of the situation. The experience itself is a horror but also leaves an impact on some of us.

Whenever we experience any sound, image, or similar situation, we start re-experiencing the incident that occurred in the past, known as a stressful post-traumatic experience. This becomes a problem in daily life because the person suffering from it starts avoiding certain areas, sounds, images, etc., limiting activity.

Life cannot be lived fully like this, and all these problems are managed when the right kind of help is taken. The help of a psychologist by taking therapy and talking with friends makes things easier to cope with.

All these things will make you slowly realize that the incidents will not happen again because you are not the same person you were in that situation. We become stronger with time but do not realize it in such situations. Learning that the problems that happened in the past will not happen again and can be left in the past will decrease the bitterness and lead you toward a happier life.

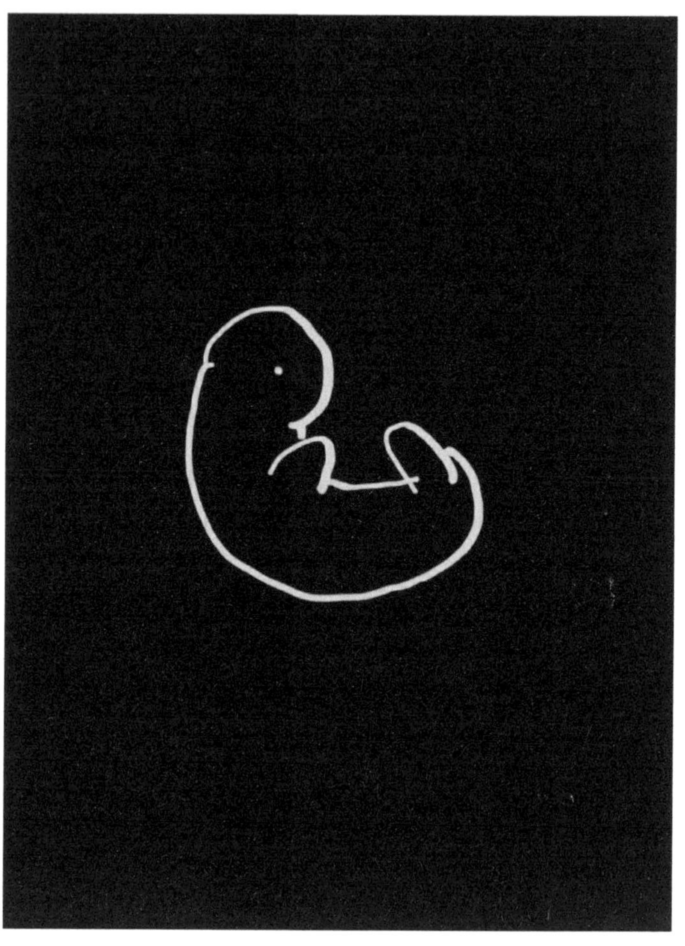

CHAPTER TWO

GUILT

> *"Only a fool is interested in other people's guilt since he cannot alter it. The wise man learns only from his guilt - Carl Jung."*

Guilt is a natural human emotion that arises when we feel we have done something wrong. We have not lived up to our own or someone else's expectations.

A little bit of guilt can be healthy and motivate us to improve our behaviour in the future. However, excessive guilt can be harmful and lead to negative consequences. These can be anxiety, low self-esteem, and depression. Some causes of extreme guilt include unrealistic expectations from self or others, trauma or abuse, cultural or religious beliefs, lack of self-compassion, and perfectionism.

On looking closely, guilt is an emotion related to the past. The things one might have done in the past or have been shamed for by others. The evolution of the human mind has invented conflict. We can no longer straightly do what our heart desires like other animals. This conflict makes us feel crippled to do things we desire. Our mind creates this emotion to prevent us from doing things that might hurt others. Man must have learned a lot by hurting during this process over thousands of years. It is crucial here to understand that humans have learned to live together in evolution. We started by making tribes that have evolved into present-day society. In earlier times, being thrown away from the tribe was equivalent to death. This feeling of guilt has its ancestral relation to this feeling of being left alone and becoming prone to death.

That's why this emotion is so vital if you start understanding that it is being used to make you do things that are acceptable to society to maintain the structure of society. To ensure that you do not break its rules apart for your desires.

It is essential to have guilt to a certain extent, and it cannot be erased from our minds completely. It can be considered reasonable to the extent of not harming anybody.

On the other extent, your guilt can be used to control you. One has to be careful about being used by others as guilt is a strong emotion, and people around you can easily manipulate you using it. The problem increases when the people using your guilt against you are the people you love.

How can people whom I love and who love me do it?

No, it's not bullshit, and this happens in reality. The people may not know that they are doing it as they may not know the boundaries to govern your life.

Man deeply desires to control other humans, rooted in the past. Slavery, ruling over one race, wars, etc., are great examples. Man has lived through a lot of unrest due to wars. Only the last century has been known in the history of humankind, where slavery and wars have come to rest. It still exists in some minor forms where some unrest is going in the present.

Only until the last few decades has the problem of individuals become essential. It was mostly about survival till now. The last few decades have been important in history. We have worked on the interest of human rights and an individual's feelings.

Our parents have not seen the amount of freedom and connectivity we are aware of. Suppose you talk to them about the psychological aspects and happiness. They will give you answers suggesting that it was unnecessary for them. They were busy with the family's survival. It is a harsh reality, but they might not be able to realise it in the future also. Man can only understand through experiences. They have somehow given up on their freedom for the more significant benefit of their family, including you. They do not know the psychological boundaries and might invade your privacy and choices. That is where control begins, and happiness dies.

Now arises the question of whether they love you or not. One can easily use this statement against their near ones. This problem can only be adequately addressed if we know our perception of others. Most of the time, our brain tricks us into making our dear ones evil to get things done, which the brain desires.

One of the correct answers to this problem is time. Nobody can fake for long, and you will eventually discover whether people care about you. Even if people around you love you, using guilt as a medium to get something done is not the right thing to do.

You will have to learn the concept of boundaries. You have to set boundaries so that you can love them freely without endangering your own choices. This is a big responsibility because we have to be very sure of ourselves.

A good company of friends or a good therapist may help you. Take their help to get insight into whether you are on the right path of thinking.

Remember, there is a potential of you taking their advantage by using this, and that is also not the right thing to do. I would say it is as difficult as walking on a thin thread. You have to create ultimate balance to make the right decisions. Remember that guilt is normal, but excessive guilt can be harmful. Practice self-compassion and seek support when needed.

CHAPTER THREE

ANXIETY

> "*No amount of anxiety is going to make any difference in anything that is going to happen -Alan Watts.*"

Anxiety is a natural human emotion. It arises when we feel threatened or overwhelmed. In the past, when humans lived in the wild and protected themselves from predators. On encountering one, the immediate response was to run away from it.

The response is also known as the fright, flight, and fight response. This response can also be understood when a dog starts barking and following you.

What will you do?

You will first sense the fear (fright) and either run away (flight). If you have some weapon in hand and feel confident enough, you might try to defend yourself (fight).

In these moments, the adrenal gland on the kidneys releases adrenaline hormones. It increases your heart rate, blood pressure, and blood glucose levels. All the energy in the body is shifted toward the brain and muscles. It makes you aware of the surroundings and runs faster or fights.

Man has worked very hard to decrease these situations. We do not get into these situations daily, and there is no need to run anymore with the advent of high-demanding and stressful schools, colleges, and jobs. This response gets ON whenever you feel you will get hurt physically or mentally.

On thinking about whether we will pass the exams, our job performance, etc., heart rate, blood pressure, and blood glucose stays raised. These stressors give us a signal similar to encountering a predator. Still, we do not do any physical activity but end up with a less working brain capacity and shivering muscles. This makes doing any action difficult.

Increased stress has caused an increase in diabetes and hypertension among young individuals. This is growing at an alarming rate and needs attention. You must understand that you are responsible for your health. You'll need to learn methods to shut down this response system independently.

Anxiety seems to be a symbol of events that will occur in the future compared to guilt related to past experiences. Both these problems have a solution by staying focused on the present moment.

There are a few things that lead to anxiety. To start with, perfectionism, when we think about doing anything, we want to make it perfect.

Why?

Because of the fear of embarrassment. When you start doing something, you will notice that the brain will try thinking about the outcome. The brain is a highly evolved organ that tries to calculate if the energy being utilized is useful. If the outcome is not good, you will have to do something that will make you stop doing the work. First, starting the work will be problematic. The brain wants its energy to be utilized only for survival. Suppose you manage to start the work by promising him more comfort in some way. It will keep calculating the outcome. During the work, if you feel the outcome will fail to be good. The brain will create visuals of embarrassment and shame, making you stop doing the work. If you still try to force or if there is no option of stopping. The fright, flight, and fight mechanisms will take over. You will start losing control over your brain and muscles. This is the reason that most of the projects keep lying on the waitlist. We need to work on meaningful work. The idea of being perfect in our work makes us worse. It is better to start thinking of ourselves as ordinary people. To keep less expectation out of our results. We have to keep telling ourselves that the outcome will be average. This calms our nerves and helps us maintain the flow of work.

Anxiety also manifests when dealing with multiple problems at once. Most of us are capable of coping with problems when they come one by one. When a person faces multiple problems at once, it becomes difficult to understand what is happening. Solving the problems all at once has a high chance that one will be unable to deal with them. While if the problems are identified as multiple and sorted to be tackled individually, it will become easier to solve them.

Another problem is multitasking, productivity, and doing things at high speed. You can try to do things faster than your brain can process. You will feel that it is not done correctly, increasing anxiety. It is essential to understand that by doing things slowly at a comfortable pace of your brain. Anxiety decreases, and your brain starts helping you by increasing focus and reducing mistakes. Multitasking is a myth; our brains are designed to focus on one thing simultaneously. Thinking about doing multiple things at a time lands us in a situation where nothing is done correctly. Productivity is being sold in every form. People seem to worry more about feeling productive than actually doing the work. It looks like a big scam as more and more people are trying to sell courses and apps on productivity. In the long run, you will realize that thinking more about productivity and less about the work increases your anxiety and dulls your thinking. With this, we can conclude that both the emotions of guilt and anxiety are only good up to some extent, after which they start harming us.

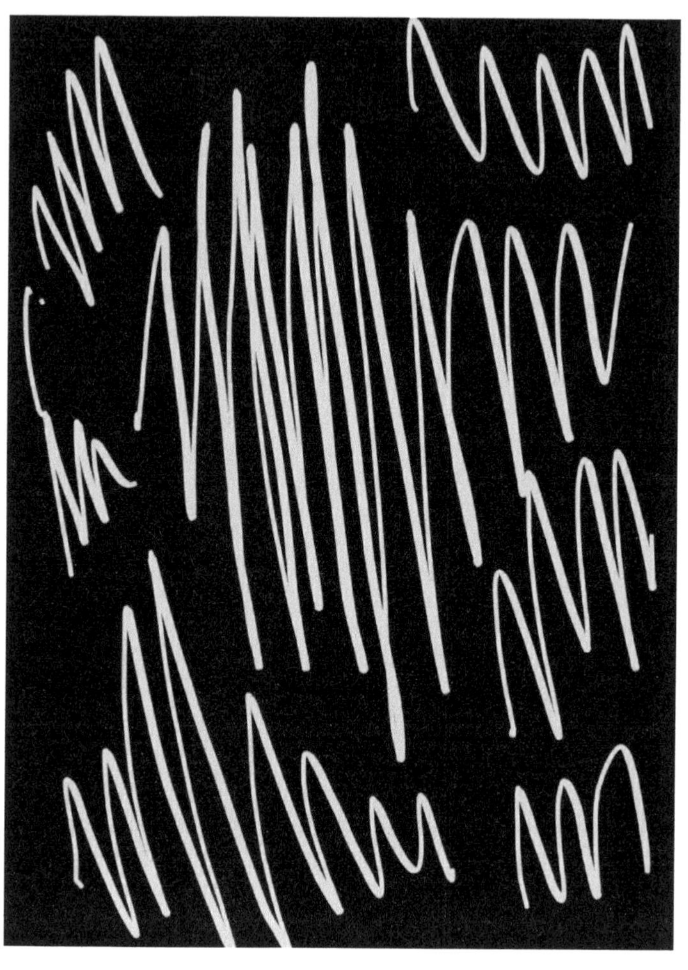

CHAPTER FOUR

ANGER

"Where there is anger, there will always be pain underneath - Echart Tolle"

"Your mind is like this water, my friend. When it is agitated, it becomes difficult to see. But if you allow it to settle, the answer becomes clear - Oogway, Kun fu panda."

Anger kills joy. It is wisely said that you only harm one person when you are angry, and that is you. Why do we get angry?

When someone says something that hurts our feelings and makes us feel we are no longer in control of the situation.

When your desires are not fulfilled when self-esteem is harmed.

Anger comes by itself. It is a natural response, an expression of the pain that you are suffering from. Sometimes the word comes in tears when you think you can't do anything. However, if you feel you have any power to retaliate, the expression comes out in a burst of anger.

Most of us cannot control it. We are always asked to control it. But then it becomes a misery.

How much anger is healthy?

How and to what extent can we prevent it?

Is there a way to avoid it?

Why do you think you can control it?

Well, it's not easy at all. But there is a way you can minimise the damage caused by it.

Damage? To whom?

Yes, the damage occurs to yourself only. The fight goes on in your mind only. Others are not aware of it. You make others aware of it by saying something back which hurts them. This results in fights. Fights, in which everybody loses—especially the angrier ones. Uncontrolled emotions can destroy the world. Especially your world. Think about it.

The first way to improve and gain control is by understanding what made you angry. It is primarily a situation where you have lost control over your self-esteem or emotion. Think about it.

Why does it happen?

Who said those words?

Sit back and don't move. Let it pass., let the storm pass, and keep observing your thoughts and emotions without reacting.

What will happen if you don't do it?

Well, either you will respond in a way that will harm you or others. It will permanently scar your condition, self-worth, or reputation. So, observe your thoughts and emotions until you understand you have been hurt. Detach yourself from those feelings. Realise that you can survive without that image you created earlier for yourself and have been torn by somebody to hurt you.

It is hard work. It isn't easy, and most people fall prey to it.

To preserve your integrity and your peace of mind. You will not let it leave a permanent mark. You will not let it define you. But you, my friend, will find your way to deal with it.

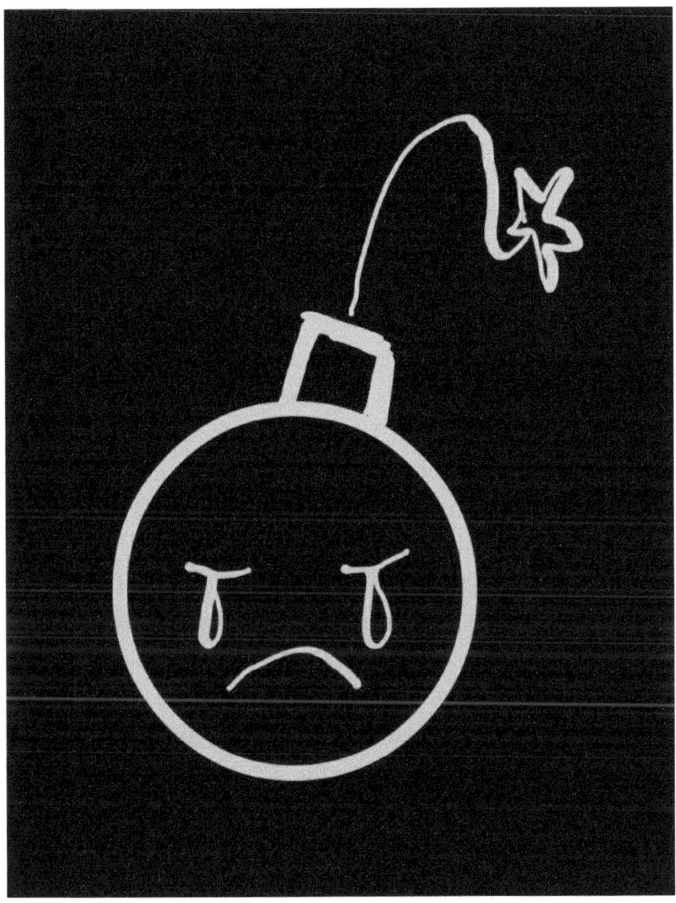

CHAPTER FIVE

JEALOUSY

"He who envies others does not obtain peace of mind - Buddha"

Jealousy is a complex emotion to deal with. It both triggers anger and guilt and confuses us about our self-worth. You will compare a person's possessions (health, wealth, relationships, knowledge) to yours. It will induce the emotion of being behind in the race of life, decrease your self-confidence, trigger anger, and finally, may start feeling bad about having all these emotions.

It is all a play between EGO and instinctual drive. Ego tells you to be a good person, and instinctual drive asks you to cheat while nobody is watching. This creates a conflict, and conflicts are never comfortable.

A war is going on inside, and the only person who will get harmed is you because you are fighting yourself. It would be best if you tried to resolve most of your conflicts to live a peaceful life. Here we have to learn the art of letting go.

When you desire something, you feel a strong urge to get it. We stop thinking about the journey one has to take to reach it. We also stop thinking about the journey that other people would have taken and the hard work that person would have put in to achieve what he has today.

To answer the emotion of jealousy, you will have to let go of the desire to possess these things in the immediate future. Then, it would help if you tried to realise the amount of work required to achieve these things.

In the case of a loving relationship, you may not get the same person even when you try as much as you can. In such situations, you should let go of the person of desire and realise that other similar options should be available.

In saying all this, I also understand your condition and feelings. Dealing with jealousy will not be easy for you or the person you are jealous of. It would help if you understood that is a normal emotion every person on this earth has.

Your ego will say you are terrible because you are jealous. You have to become compassionate towards yourself and feel normal. It will make things easier for you.

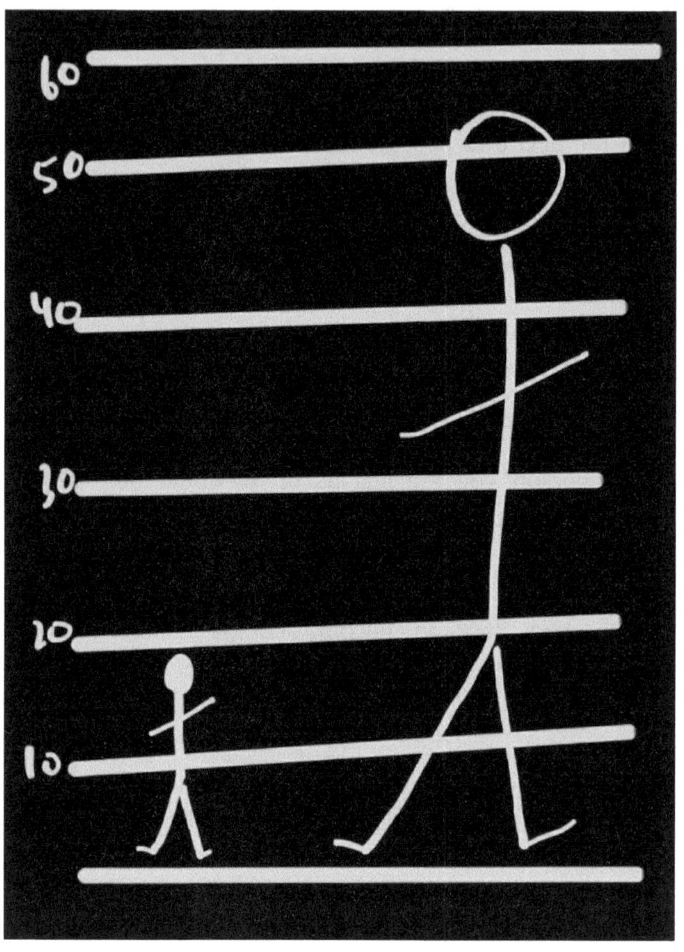
60
50
40
30
20
10

CHAPTER SIX

NUMBNESS

The person who experiences all this usually lands into neurotic problems like lower self-esteem, anxiety, and guilt. These conditions become a problem when they are trying to do something good with their life.

Many individuals fall into addictions like alcohol, smoking, drugs, food, gaming, etc. These addictions may help numb the pain initially. They significantly impact the happiness and career of these individuals

> "*Numbing the pain for a while will make it worse when you finally feel it - JK Rowling.*"

Life is full of uncomfortable things. When we learn new things, face people we don't like, and do difficult things, it creates a feeling of discomfort. Man has been building a lifestyle ever since in which he doesn't have to be uncomfortable.

Whenever we face situations that endanger the comfort status in our minds, we tend to avoid these situations. These situations range from reading up for an exam, going to the gym, and completing an important project.

All such sort of things brings the fear of failure and embarrassment. To avoid feeling this fear, one has to get detached from it. We indulge in entertainment to numb ourselves.

We invented entertainment to derail ourselves from the thoughts of fear, pain, and loneliness. Most people are seen as indulging in watching TV, gaming, alcohol, smoking, or doing something else which kills time.

However, it is easy for others to judge somebody who indulges in all these addictions. The actual need in this situation is to look at the person in pain behind all this.

We are all afraid of doing something which brings us discomfort.

Does this mean that these addictions are natural?

Yes, they are! They are the result of a reflex of the brain to protect itself from difficult situations.

Does it help us?

Yes, initially, but not in the long run.

The person who is indulged in all this draws attention from the problems and wastes much valuable time. This time could have been used to solve the issues.

By utilising the time, we can do things required and expected of us.

Is it possible to stop wasting time on entertainment to numb pain and fear?

It is difficult to face and solve emotional problems. The normal tendency is to sway away from them and numb the pain.

It is not easy to prevent falling prey to procrastination from feeling pain. Still, it is possible to develop a habit of realising earlier that you are in the process of procrastination and stopping it when you realise it.

Nobody will be able to do it for you. Any form of engagement in the present moment helps in coming out of it. Exercising, walking, meditating, playing a sport, etc., can help you connect with the present.

I would emphasise certain activities that are specific to the individual. You have been doing these activities out of love and for a long time. In most cases, these things are your hobbies.

If you can manage to get yourself to do these things, they will bring comfort and strength back, and you will gain your confidence back.

Having attained your power back, you can start trying to solve the problem which made you procrastinate. Understanding this problem of coming out of entertainment and procrastination will make you focus more on the problem at hand and work on the problem to solve it.

Doing this will slowly make you stronger and decrease problems in your life.

CHAPTER SEVEN

FORGIVENESS

I came from a problematic family and faced many of these problems. I started hating the people who were responsible. It did not bring any solution and increased the pain. We cannot live happily while keeping hatred for anybody in our hearts. I had to forgive them for whatever happened in my past, and this activity made me a happier person. It was not an easy task.

I saw a lot of documentaries on people who were abused in some way or other in their lives.

Anger towards the person who did all this to these children makes them bitter in adulthood. It becomes difficult to trust people. Trust is essential to build good relationships. These individuals have problems developing deeper relationships with their friends and spouse.

During world war 2, Jews were kept in concentration camps by Nazis. They were enslaved as experimental guinea pigs and killed in gas chambers. This is an example of inhuman and extreme torture in human history after the war's end. Many Jew prisoners were rescued. Survivors of the camp developed neurotic problems after being rescued. Some of them found a way to live happily. Two twin sisters were used for medical experiments in the centre. They underwent many medical interventions by a Nazi doctor in the camp. One of them died during the experiments. Another was rescued but was not able to walk correctly after these experiments.

She gave an interview many years after being rescued. In the interview, she talked about both suffered physical and mental torture. She told how humans were being used as guinea pigs by other humans in that era. She described how she lived in terror while dealing with experimenting on her body, how she coped with all this and finally faced the Nazi doctor who was still alive. She said she had to forgive him for her happiness as we remain, prisoners of the past if we keep hatred in our hearts.

Forgiving is the most difficult thing to do, and you might not even like this idea. But eventually, you may realise it is not worth it after burning yourself in anger for years. Forgiving makes you a better and happier person.

CHAPTER EIGHT

INNER STRENGTH

"Look for the magic in daily routines - Lou Barlow"

I was brought up by my sisters. They always took care of me, which made me an asshole. I had no habit of taking my glass of water to drink myself and will ask one of them to hand it over to me whenever I felt thirsty. They fed me while I was reading. They sacrificed their precious time. When I left home a few years back to live alone. I started doing the daily work independently. Cleaning the floor, washing dishes, buying groceries, and cooking myself. It was the most challenging time of my life. I was only programmed to do things that gave me a high about myself. These things were part of the so-called mundane life. I started getting stomach aches while doing the dishes and backache when I cleaned the floor. It was not due to any physical cause in my body but anxiety. I felt so uncomfortable doing all these things. I never did these things on my own, and due to this, I realised a fear that I was dealing with.

When you don't know the skills to survive by yourself and become dependent on others, it will create fear. There is a feeling of not having control over your life. I felt I would not be able to live alone. This further creates a hidden fear of separation from those caring for you.

If they care for you, this person is usually your mother, father, and sometimes siblings. If one is lucky to have parents and siblings who care, this problem is benign. But most of us don't know what people want from us.

This dependence on people makes us weak while making decisions when these people want us to do something wrong. It might not be excellent for you to hear. Most of you would not have faced a situation till now, but it will be easier for those who have gone through this. The rest of us will probably face this in the future.

So, by understanding the grave nature of this problem. We should start inculcating the habit of becoming independent in these survival routines. We all should live away from home to create an environment of loneliness.

Inner strength comes by itself when you are not dependent on anybody, especially for the basic necessities of life. Inner strength comes from practising these things on a regular basis so that they become your integral part. Like a martial artist practices his kicks, you should practice your chores daily. It all starts with waking up early and making your bed. Learning to become independent with your food. Learning to reach your workplace on time etc. It's all the mundane and boring part of your day which makes you reach a step towards your goals.

Doing these chores will be painful at first. Once you develop the habits, it will remove the fear of loneliness if you stand up for your thoughts. Otherwise, your thoughts will succumb to your fears. Hence, you must become independent in self-care and chores to develop a strong character.

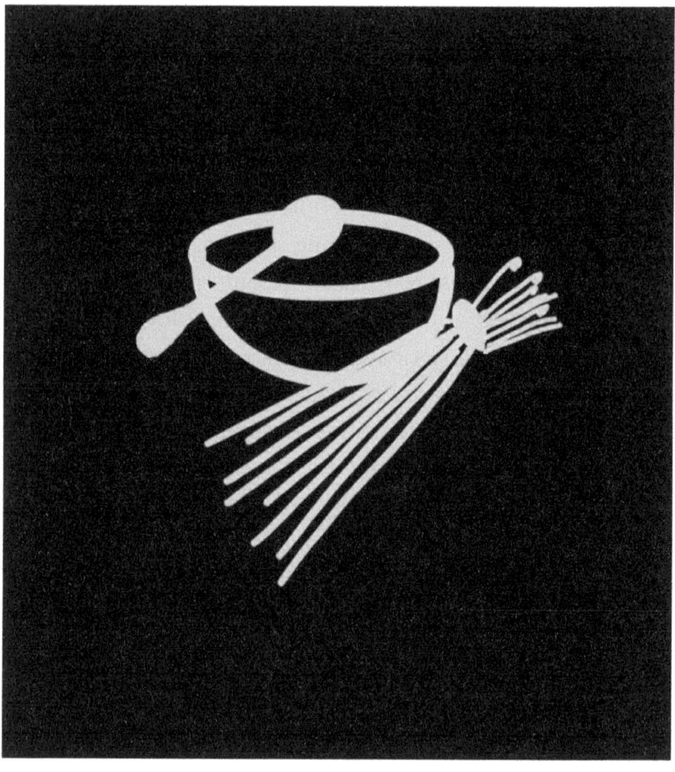

CHAPTER NINE

FEAR

"The biggest fear of man is to become himself - Batman begins"

Everybody is running after the perfect life. Everybody wants a college degree, a well-paying job, a trophy like a husband or a wife, respect in society, a house, and vehicles. All these things are called materialistic success. They are essential as modern man can only stay away from these things for a short time.

The problem arises when you start compromising on more valuable things in return. These more valuable things are your health, Loving and meaningful relationships, self-worth, your honesty with yourself and others.

The reason for this bargain is comparison. You see others having more than you, and you feel jealous. With upgrading technology, the problem is increasing. All social media and its marketing are built around your feeling of self-worth.

The people in business know that to make you buy something you don't need, they must first develop your need. The first step in marketing is making the customer realize that they don't have the product being sold.

Toothpaste ads will tell you your teeth are not white enough; detergents will say to you your clothes are not clean enough, and beauty product ads will show you that you don't look like the model they recruited.

They will not tell you that this model suffers from anorexia nervosa due to her dieting. They spend 4 hours a day in the gym and the rest of the time caring for their skin. Undergo many plastic surgeries. Deal with a lot of mental trauma to get this look. They struggle in the rest of the blocks of their life in which they are doing good.

They will show you ads of cars with female models to take advantage of your loneliness and lust. Your brain won't perceive this is happening. You will spend a lot unnecessarily and make wrong financial decisions to fulfill your emotions. People will label you stupid, but these people will also fall prey to some of these traps.

They will take advantage of your poverty and make false promises to you. They will offer you dreams of becoming rich in a few days or months and make you buy programs/ courses. Most people end up losing money and blaming themselves for their failure.

You will compete in school to become a topper. If you don't succeed, you will live your life thinking that you are not good enough. Students pay a hefty amount of tuition fees in coaching classes and, in the end, blame themselves for being lazy if they do not get desired results.

The list of such things is endless. If you reach the top, you will meet people who used all sorts of unfair means to win. Corruption is present in everything, whether studying in schools or colleges, finding jobs, or doing business.

Most people fall prey to the system and give up their pure hearts and honesty to become part of it. You will bribe, cheat and take advantage of people experiencing poverty. The only thing that will make you do all this is fear.

Fear of judgment, failure, and not being accepted in society. Humankind has developed a habit of becoming a part of something bigger than itself.

We feel small and powerless when we are alone. Everybody wants prefix and suffix names attached to their names in the form of degrees and posts. Everybody wants to be part of a bigger organization which makes them feel accomplished. Everybody is afraid.

Everybody wants to find a loving spouse, but it adds many complications. First, the other person you want to be in a relationship with has to look good. Looking good here means fitting into the stereotype society has created. Then your parents will tell you that you must adjust to your emotions. You can select only among a few people due to religious and cast based restrictions. After this will come the difference between monetary status and whatnot. You will end up with only one or two options to choose from. You will eventually hate your spouse and parents if things don't turn out well. Most people end up lonely, feeling stupid, and broke.

Only a few of us win the so-called race to realize they did not get what they sought. This feeling makes them indulge in drugs to numb their loneliness and despair. The drugs and alcohol calm their nerves for a duration. But the need for increased dose and decreased effect worsens over time.

It is time you realize all this is happening and tries to open your eyes to find the answer "Why you were given this life." It must not be about winning or losing in a race you don't want.

The question should be answered, as nature does not create things without purpose. It evolves itself, and evolution depends on the curiosity of nature to find the need and correct it.

You must understand that you are a part of this nature and universe. You have to find your place and purpose to exist rather than just following the crowd. Stay away from going after something you don't even know if you want.

To come out of the race, you have to unlearn what has been told to you by the world since childhood. You don't have to fit yourself into the stereotypical image of a successful person.

You have to find the things that bring joy to you.

It is not about money or status but what makes you feel like you can do this all day without boredom.

There will be no corruption if everybody does what they love to do. Whether you earn out of it or not will matter to you. - Jiddu Krishnamurti

CHAPTER TEN

Pain & Loneliness

What is loneliness?

Is it merely the absence of people around you?

Or is it feeling lonely even when surrounded by your loved ones?

Have you experienced it?

Do you know that this can happen?

I'm sure some of you might have experienced it. I have been in it for quite a long time.

I have a loving family and a friend who loves me more than a brother.

I completed my studies in 2021. In 2016 I completed my under graduation and started preparing to become a specialist doctor. There were some issues at home, so I had to leave home to achieve peace of mind to study. This was the first time when I was living away from home. My younger sister came along with me to look for her career. Also, In 2016, I broke up with my longtime girlfriend, But I somehow buried the pain to prepare for my exams.

2017 was the most challenging year so far.

I was selected for the residency program in 2018 and started working. The first year of residency was tough. I lost the love from my family that I usually get ever since childhood. In India, you don't get time to think about even basic necessities like food and clothing in junior residency, especially in the first year due to a busy work schedule. In my senior year of residency, I started getting free early. That was the first time I had time to think about myself and what had happened to me in the last 2 to 3 years.

I started thinking about the loss of my Ex girlfriend and the love from my family, which happened in the past couple of years. I lived with my friend and sister. Both of them were available for me whenever I needed them. Initially, in my senior years, I was feeling relieved from the burden of work, but slowly, I started to feel an emptiness. I started to stay entirely away from conversations with my sister and friend. There was something that I couldn't tell them. I was missing her but was not able to voice it out. I felt a void in my heart that was not filling up with anything. I used to cry when nobody was around. Initially, I was unable to make out what was happening to me. I just felt alone no matter what. My sister and friend tried to talk, but I didn't respond. Soon I started avoiding any conversations with anybody as it grew on me.

I started losing interest in everything. Be it work, a company of friends, or anything you can name. It felt like I had dug up a well for myself and closed it from every corner. I was not letting anyone in. Then it became worse. Suicidal thoughts started coming into my mind. Life started feeling meaningless. I was listening to many speakers at that time. I was also trying to escape it in my way. I had access to therapy, but I was afraid of saying anything to anyone, So I did it alone. I started finding answers to loneliness and came across many concepts. The most beautiful answers to my problems were said by Jiddu Krishnamurti. He had talked about almost every aspect of life. I came across two of his books related to love and loneliness. It was those books that helped me crawl out of my loneliness slowly.

The answers that helped me understand my condition were simple but hard to digest and follow. While reading those books, I realised how I was growing up with the wall around me and how I was making it difficult for my loved ones to reach me. I slowly stopped staying away from my friend and sister. I learned to love others even when empty and started feeling better about myself again. It was not easy, but I wish a small help to understand my situation could have helped me overcome it earlier at that time. I hope somebody who reads this gets help from my little story on loneliness.

Start accepting your feelings, even if they are unbearable. The feeling will remain there even if you ignore them or get scared of them.

Try to see where they are coming from... try to find the reason.

Try to understand and realize that you are increasing the distance from those who love you.

Love back people who love you as they are irreplaceable, and your only hope to survive this situation.

Life is about forgiving others for things people do unintentionally. Try finding out if you are not forgiving your loved ones for small things, as every person makes mistakes. If you start finding fault in small things, you will end up disliking people and loneliness.

Even the best ones will unintentionally break your heart and hurt you with silly mistakes.

Only love and forgiveness will help in such a situation. Try to see how they forgive the tremendous mistakes you make.

I am sure you can come out of your Void this way. And yes, don't hesitate to take therapy if you find it challenging to handle on your own

"*It is beautiful to be alone. To be alone does not mean to be lonely. It means the mind is not influenced and contaminated by society - Jiddu Krishnamurti.*"

CHAPTER ELEVEN

SPIRAL

Have you ever tried to observe the nature of life?

Do you see any repeating pattern?

Do you experience similar situations one after another?

Life gives second chances, and it may be due to the structure of life. Initially, life seems like a straight line from birth to death, but many theories have suggested a circular pattern. However, looking closely, you will observe that it is a spiral. You come to see a similar situation but with subtle changes.

You are more mature when you reach a similar situation. You can make better decisions and sometimes overcome regrets also. If you consider this maturity as moving towards a centre, the path becomes a spiral. Thus, the journey has a course toward the centre, and you are moving closer to your inner self. Strange, but so hopeful. Because if you look at it this way, you will have a chance to correct your past mistakes and overcome regrets. Without hope, life seems unfair and useless. Moving on a spiritual journey makes you realise it is more about finding peach inwards. We never look inside ourselves to find peace. That is why people go to places to find it. You don't need to go anywhere. You don't have to seek anybody but yourself. All the answers are within. All the things you need are within yourself. You have to start looking for them inside and trust yourself.

You keep coming back to find the deeper truth

CHAPTER TWELVE

SPIRIT

"*To be alive spiritually, man must have a union with God and must be conscious of it. Apart from this union, his religious life will be an empty drudgery, a mere imitation of true spirituality - Alan Watts*"

I heard about the word spirituality in my twenties. The term should be discussed more in better sections of society and among youngsters. I was attracted to this word because I found hope of finding god through it, probably, which was one of my curiosities.

When we enter the world of spirituality, We imagine seeing people with white clothes, garlands of flowers, and serene face which shines with the glory of eternal peace.

How do people attain such calmness?

At first, I confused it with religious practices. Later, it appeared more about finding your position in the universe's structure and becoming one. Spirituality is a relationship you establish between yourself and your soul, your inner voice, and your self. I was always fond of some of my teachers in college who radiated such kind of energy. They were young at heart. They cared less about the outer world and delivered their service with a pure heart to the students.

I always wondered if such humans are born this way or if they made themselves into such creatures. Seeing them was a love affair, and I always wanted to become like them. There was no natural way available to be able to discuss it with them freely. It remained a distant love affair only.

I started finding people who were like them and did such great work that people wrote documentaries on their lives. Some favorites are APJ Abdul Kalam, Mother Teresa, and His Holiness, The Dalai Lama.

I learned about Islamic, Buddhist, Hindu, Christian, and Taoist religious practices and beliefs. I tried to understand their relationship with spirituality. All this gave me a glimpse of the idea of what exists.

I began meditation five years ago and practiced it for hours daily. Slowly I learned about different forms of meditation and started practicing awareness during every activity. Everything became part of being one with the present moment, from washing dishes to walking.

In one year, I started seeing changes in consciousness. I did not believe the sudden changes, but they were ecstatic. The things which were annoying and frustrating earlier became funny. I started understanding my relationship with everything around me and felt one with it.

I don't know whether it is some game that your mind plays with you, but it makes you a better version of yourself. It can be called a journey in which you learn more about yourself. Your beliefs, desires, and the structure of your mind, which you have built slowly since childhood. You know about past trauma and how it affects your present. Your regrets and how they control your emotions. Your unaddressed desires are repressed and enormously waiting for a chance to explore and come out.

It is not easy because we are running away from all this. Giving your attention to these things make it uneasy but opens the door to correction of the mistakes of the past. It opens the gateway to forgiving yourself and others who were responsible for putting you into such a condition.

Peace is attained when you clear out all the things you have slid under the bed without clearing them. It is essential to living with a light heart without all this heavy baggage. Living a single day in peace after earning all this makes you fulfilled and stop fearing the end.

When the fear goes away, you meet your actual self. The person you were before the world started creating its impact on you like an innocent child with no hatred, no regrets. Only love will flow from your heart towards every living being and yourself. Living a single moment in such serenity will make you feel relieved. You will understand your relationship with this eternal universe.

You will not need people to fill your loneliness, but you will fill up the void of love in the life of people around you.

CHAPTER THIRTEEN

FOCUS

"The successful warrior is the average man with laser-like focus
- Bruce Lee"

Meditation helps increase focus. It is not a way to practice and attain something related to the higher being. It is just a tool that helps us create a habit of returning to the present moment. There are different types of meditation, but the most commonly done is the one where you practice breathing in and out.

It seems easy, but we start noticing something we are unaware of as we go deeper. We realize how difficult it is to concentrate just on the breath. In a few seconds, your mind will jump to a thought. It can be any thought which might be already present in your mind due to your current circumstances. It might be a newly made thought which is irrelevant to the mind.

You will return to the breath, but it will go stray again. It will frustrate you to see how fragile your concentration is and how easily you can get distracted by your mind, even if you are sitting alone in a dark room without distractions.

At first, I left it for a while because it worsened my life. The thoughts that were coming were annoying and sometimes decreased my self-worth also. I had no choice but to return to meditation because I wanted to learn it. I habitually returned to the breath more frequently with time and got less frustrated. To me, it was a moment of astonishment that the lesson is to learn how not to get frustrated.

The more you do it, the more your thoughts run away. Slowly you start taking it as a funny game because you cannot stop your thoughts from originating, as it distracts you from focusing on the breath. I started enjoying it. When something annoyed me, I began to take my attention away from it and toward the task. Thus, it helped decrease my frustration with life also. It did help me. Slowly my concentration grew, and I could focus more on my daily activities.

I learned different forms of meditation, which increase your compassion towards the other people around you. I learned to meditate while washing dishes and walking. Later, I realized I did it unintentionally during my surgeries since I am a working doctor and saw what many people missed.

I do not practice sitting meditation anymore, but it has been ingrained in my personality to leave things I cannot control and focus more on what I can.

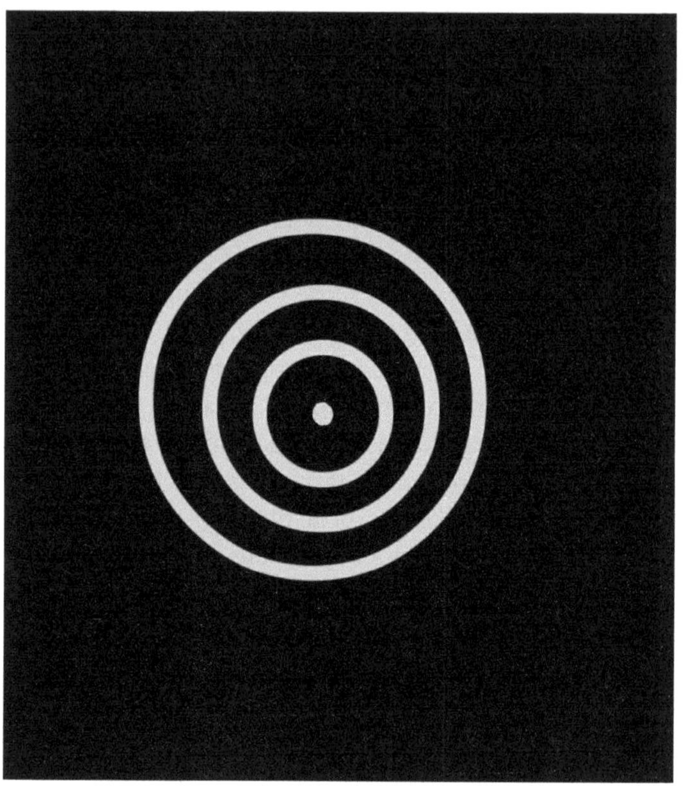

CHAPTER FOURTEEN

UNDESIRED

What is Ego?

First, we must understand it because most people confuse it with grandiosity. EGO and ID govern humans. When we are born, we do not have any ego. All living beings have ID (Instinctual Drive), which governs our behaviour. When a child is hungry, it wants to eat. The urge to eat when hungry is very strong. Slowly the child attains sexual Drive, which matures in adolescence. It is powerful but cannot be expressed simply as eating food. In earlier times when we didn't have formed society and rules. The adolescent would have indulged in sexual practices, which would have satisfied their need to turn the sexual urge off.

Nature has designed this Drive in a way to sustain the repopulation of the earth by living beings. Humans are the only living beings who have tried to put restrictions on it. We do not allow one to express their sexual emotions freely. We probably faced many problems because of it. We started living in an organised system of society. It is complicated to express this energy in a formed society freely. Forming a system to prevent it and protect the community was essential for the survival of society. We are at a stage where people refrain from discussing sexual

Drive, desire, and behaviour. Children are unknowingly told that thinking about and talking about is terrible. Adults are taught that being celibate is superior. Hundreds of stories of saints were celibate and regarded as superior human beings and closer to god than we are. Every religion teaches us that sexual Drive is a bad energy and we have to control it.

What is the price that we pay for it?

It never leaves us and comes out in uglier ways. We try to repress repeated thoughts and lose all our energy in fighting this war we have started in ourselves. In a talk by Jiddu Krishnamurti, he tells stories of Yogis who refrained from it for 15- 20 years and, in the end, admitted that they could not come over it. Many religious leaders are caught in illegal sexual practices, rapes, and whatnot. Still, all this has not opened our eyes to the failure of this system to kill the desire. Some of the talks by many spiritual teachers tell how sexual desire increases if you try to suppress it. Young unmarried adults are advised not to masturbate. Many evils have been attached to masturbation by almost all religions which makes these adolescents and young adults confused. They develop various kinds of neurotic problems. Thoughts cannot be stopped, and there is no way to get relief. Sex before marriage is prohibited, and finding a good partner for marriage is difficult. Also, for a wedding, one has to be stable in providing for a family for which one has to make a career and earn enough, which makes them reach the age of 25 to 30. Mature sexual Drive, which starts at 12 to 13 years of age, stays for around 10 to 15 years until it finds a way. But till then, it is mainly governed by anxiety, depression, and other neurotic conditions. Sigmund Freud upon the impact of this energy on our lives and behaviour. I don't think the world has taken it seriously enough to understand its effects. We underestimate the impact of the development of psychological abnormalities due to repressing these emotions. Individuals should be free to learn how to balance it in their lives. Not at the cost of another person but to learn a healthy way by understanding that it is a part of our being, like we need food when we get hungry.

Do you fear yourself?

Has anything happened to you and felt the loss of control over yourself in some situations?

Man has two psychological personalities that govern actions. Instinctual drive (Drive) is the urge to kill, eat, have sex, and all your negative emotions since birth. These are present in every animal to help in the survival of the individual and species. It's an energy that doesn't differentiate between your loved ones and others. It carries all the negative energy one can think of. Understandably, such an amount of power cannot be stored in a body that lives in a formed society system that we live in. We have forgotten that humans are, at the core, not more than other animals when it comes to the Drive. But to live in society, a person must restrict this personality's activities. Here comes the role of the Ego. A person's Ego is not powerful enough to the extent that it can initially stop the monstrous energy of Drive during childhood. The Ego gets stronger by experiences where you are punished for doing what the Drive wants you to do.

When you break something in childhood, you are punished. When we do some act that is prohibited, we are punished. We get stomach pain when we overeat. Family and friends do not accept us if we do something that is not allowed. In this way, the Ego takes its role to counterbalance the work of Drive to prevent you from falling into situations of punishment. Here the emotion of guilt takes birth. It makes you feel bad when you do something that is not allowed, and outside punishment is not required after a certain age.

With time you learn to balance the action of the Ego and drive. However, because of specific examples, most people have developed dysregulation of this system. The system of creating an Ego became more complicated. The saintly repressed their desires to such an extent that made peer pressure on humans almost killed all the activity of Drive. The children and young adults are taught directly to repress all emotions from the Drive. Such repression is necessary for the fulfilment of the desires of society to sustain itself with its wide variety of customs and rules.

But what does it take from a human by repressing the drive emotions to such an extent?

Drive, as told already, is a powerful energy. It cannot be stored or contained for more than a specific period. You can force yourself to shut it down for some time, but man has still not realised that it can grow like the Ego and balance and even surpass it. Thus, it can be easily understood that we cannot hold on for longer to contain it. Now imagine Drive, which was already an animal instinct, is growing to an extent to match the stature of a saintly ego. It turns into an equally opposite personality, equivalent to the opposite of the saint, a demon, or a monster. So we are creating the devil ourselves and then thinking about where such negative energy comes from. This demon is capable of doing anything you could ever imagine. Some of you might have chilled with fear imagining this monster inside you. You would be anxious about what will happen if it comes out. If it gets unleashed. The fear is real. We fear our demon because we know what it is capable of doing.

We start to chain ourselves because we fear it is coming out. We leash ourselves to prevent it from making us do things we don't want to. The cost of chaining yourself is a weakness. We feel weak. Full of Anxiety and guilt. We become nonfunctional individuals who torture themselves to death in our minds with the occasional outburst of Drive energy.

Have you realised why we need drugs, alcohol, disco lights, and high-volume music?

All these help us release some of the pent-up energy. But is it working?

Without healthy control, you cannot make peace with yourself. Your power is stored within the monster, and you must learn to utilise its energy without being controlled. One way is to start loving your Drive like a mistreated animal. Stop feeling bad about it and own it. Stop fearing it and try to listen to it. It will tell you the story in which it was beaten to death by you for decades. If you understand it, you might become friends with it. The movie Venom is an excellent example of how a human and a Venom alien turn their relationship into a symbiotic one. The venom gives it power and human guides it to use the energy for a good cause. It will help if you come to peace with it to learn to live with yourself completely. If you understand it, listen to its needs. You will slowly realise how it shrinks down to a tiny puppy. It will sometimes need food which is justified for even your survival and can help you achieve your great goals by giving you its power. Learn to pet your monster so you don't feel weak and frightened again.

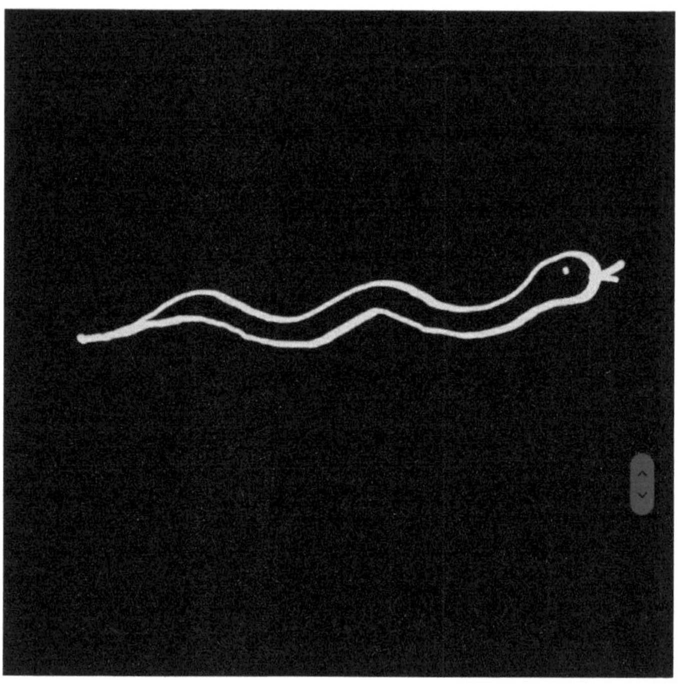

CHAPTER FIFTEEN

DESIRED

I began meditation in 2017 and did it religiously to understand myself and connect with god. I read about Buddhism and Taoism during this period. I was not able to find god anywhere. Started listening to Gurus and spiritual teachers. Nothing in my life was improving spiritually. It was a fake sense of doing something to achieve god, and I felt no real connection. I was lonely and angry. Most speakers today rely on one particular religion, which gives them the strength to appeal to the audience for their already existing faith. I listened to some Old teachers who did not participate in a religious activity but only talked about the intellect of the human being. They were well-read people who explored themselves inwardly and found the root cause of problems and their existence. These teachers never asked the listeners to rely on themselves and think about it on their own to understand whether their statements were true. All this sent me into deeper thinking; sometimes, even without meditation, I would think and find the answers myself. I realized humans feel lonely and want someone else to love, care for, and protect them. We created many things to run away from this loneliness. One of them is god. We have created god so that we could never reach or achieve it and thus keep finding him. It gives our lives a purpose. We created a fear of god. We created punishments and rewards from god if we acted in a certain way. We made it both easy and hard for ourselves. Easy because we don't have to think much about it, and hard because we put so many boundaries on ourselves. Now we exist in a world where we think a hundred times before doing anything.

Will it please god?

Will it annoy him?

It's funny to think that we made God-like ourselves. He can get angry and pleased like humans. He has the same problems we have. Our emotions control our judgment. His emotions also carry him away. However, if we think deeply, every action has a deeper meaning. Nothing can be painted black (bad) and white (good). Instead, everything in this world is grey. We want things to be black and white so that we don't have to use our brains to think about these things. This made me think that if ever a thing exists, which is the supreme power that controls this universe, it must be above this judgemental mentality to see right and wrong in living beings. Then came the question of its existence in the physical world. Being a science student, I read about the nature of the presence of particles in the universe. All of us are obsessed with the idea that god is omnipotent (present everywhere).

Then what could be why we cannot see or feel him?

Some speakers said that you calm yourself down and feel his presence. I tried that and could not find him. Carl Sagan, an astrophysicist, explained different dimensions and theories on their existence in a lecture. He explained how an organism of the 2-dimensional world could not appreciate the actual shape of a 3-dimensional object.

Similarly, if we bring the 3-dimensional creatures, we cannot see a 4-dimensional object. This idea stuck with me thinking that god could be a 4D or 5D existence which explains his access to all the places and time and our inability to perceive him. Another speaker Alan Watts says that we are god. The idea of being god creates grandiosity, but in his following line, he says that the problem arises when you think only you are god. You must understand that probably everyone is a god. How funny is that?

We must worship each other, but all wars and hatred will cease if it happens. So it made me wonder how an imperfect thing like the people around me and I can be gods. But, the idea struck me. Because it helps decrease our loneliness, it automatically brings compassion and love to the people around us. I know how to worship this god. I have to do what pleases him. It means I can do everything I love without fear and refrain from doing things other gods around me don't like.

Was it this easy?

I don't have to think about the other person's religion before talking to him, and probably he also won't if he understands.

Now it was sorted for me, and I started caring for myself. Slowly I realised I don't do it very often, and this was the cause of my misery. I don't love myself. I didn't like my company. But now I started enjoying it because I began to love myself as I loved God. I forgave myself and others for minor mistakes and started believing in myself. Life was not this easy before. It is still a theory, but it solves the problems. Being emotional, judgmental, 3D creatures, we cannot understand the existence of a supreme power that can govern us. How we try to understand him needs a proper understanding. I now feel his unjudgemental, loving presence inside me all the time, and I don't have to do anything to please him, which makes me free to do what I want and love myself.

It feels like actual freedom.

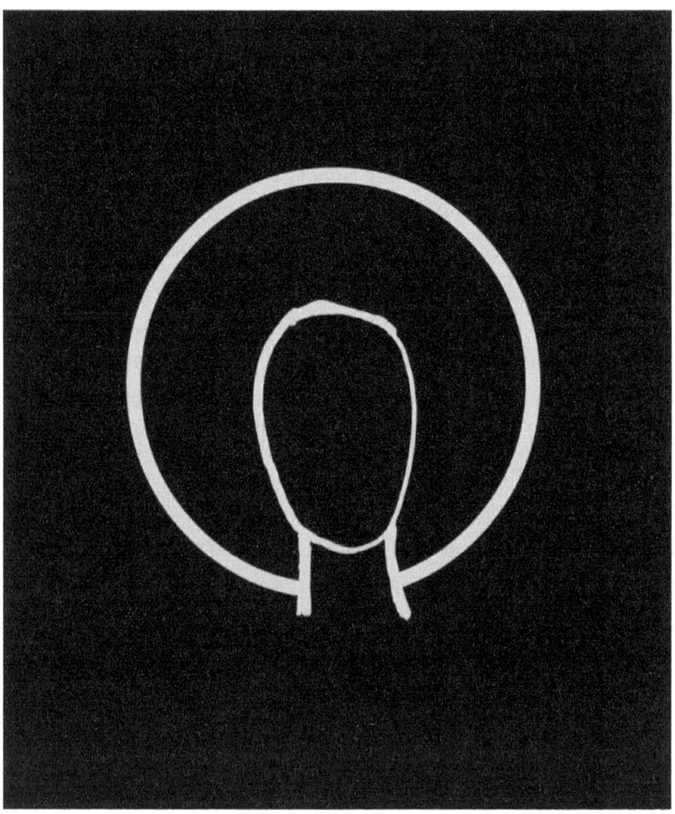

CHAPTER SIXTEEN

TRUTH

I have been hearing about finding the Truth for a long time.

But what Truth are we talking about?

Is one answer or Truth sufficient to get all the answers simultaneously?

It was a question that kept coming up repeatedly.

Will one find the ultimate Truth in god?

Will it lead to god?

All sorts of questions come to mind when you are on a spiritual journey. It was the most difficult part to understand because so many paths are laid before us, all claiming to lead to the ultimate Truth. most of these paths are in the form of religion.

Being a modern man with scientific knowledge makes it difficult to take things as they are told. The habit of questioning everything until your heart confirms that this is the right answer makes you a rebel. Much pain from life also makes you question the paths already laid. Every failure to reach the destination seems to take you closer to the right path.

Then came the line from Jiddu Krishnamurti "Truth is a pathless land" If you try to take any known path toward it, you will get lost and confused. Only the way shown by the heart can take you to the ultimate Truth of life. I'm also influenced by the speakers and some of the films and documentaries. but the closest I came to an understanding the Truth was that it is so painful and hopeless that we don't want to see it directly in the Eyes.

All the things in the world have one way of looking at them. Everything is judged differently by every other person. Still, there is just one thing that cannot be interpreted in any other way. I have been a doctor for years and have seen patients dying so frequently and closely that it has become routine. Seeing the death of near and dear ones has also opened many gateways in my mind. Maybe it's just me being sensitive toward everything and observing everything so closely. I used to fear ghosts in childhood, but after seeing many deaths, I understand their nature and process.

Being doctors, we see how people take their last breath. Sometimes in our arms. We see how pupils dilate, how the body becomes cold, how it tightens in a few hours and the body's decomposition. It seems entertaining for humans to make fun of it by thinking about ghosts and not looking at the misery and the beautiful process that takes place simultaneously. We see new babies being born into the world, taking their first breath through crying. We see how fragile life is. I think these things influenced me to think in this direction.

The Fountain (movie) plunged me into deep thinking about death and how it is inevitable.

A movie about the Dalai lama showed how his father dies, and the body is cut into pieces and fed to vultures. The moment I saw that scene shook me and made me think about my parent's death in the future, and immense pain ran throughout my body, imagining what would happen.

The next moment was serene and painful, and I understood the reality.

The Truth just came to me like a pearl found inside a shell buried in the immense ocean of pain.

"The truth is Death."

It cannot be denied. It cannot be seen in any other way. Man has built many things to evade thinking about it.

But the ultimate Truth, which cannot be changed, is that you will die someday and also see the death of your loved ones. All hope is lost after realising it, but it is a door that, when opened, awakens you. It Makes you realise what you are doing in your day-to-day life. You have only one life which you are wasting by living to please others.

Every day which is lived by not doing what you love is wasted. Every time you think about your death, all the nonsense of grandiosity, Ego, Money, Position, Power, etc., will vanish, and you will see the naked Truth of where you stand.

You will realise how lonely you are if you don't love others; you will realise that the money you are accumulating and not using to help yourself or others is wasted. You will think about the useless things you said to somebody. All you possess will be taken away from you. To cure all this, man has created the idea of reincarnation and the afterlife. They ask you to blindly believe in these ideas because they have no concrete evidence. You fear dying and going to hell.

You want to go to heaven if you die someday. But what if these things do not exist?

What if the life given to you is wasted in the process of preparing for the afterlife?

Do you imagine at what scale this fear is being sold? I rescued myself from all this by accepting this life as the end of everything and living as if there was no tomorrow. I would not say that I don't care about the future anymore, but it has decreased to the extent that it is bearable now.

What is the point of living if this is the Truth?

I found life very beautiful when I started living for myself for the first time. Not caring about what others will think about me if I marry someone society doesn't allow. If I changed my career and did what I love, my work is not working anymore, and I would feel something for it.

Suppose you live in this way by breaking all the boundaries. In that case, you will realise that life is very livable, and you can say it is a gift to those who cherish it. Doing what you love is always better than ending your life. The things that make us feel to end our lives are unnecessary things, people who don't see through our pain. It is better to leave them instead of leaving yourself.

Correspondence

You can share your views with me:
author.shahrukh@gmail.com

9 798890 265104

Printed by Libri Plureos GmbH in Hamburg, Germany